Confirmation Register

SPCK

Confirmations

Entry no.	Date of birth	Christian name(s)	Surname *In block capitals*	Address

Parish of

in the Diocese of

in the   of

Insert appropriate local government area

Date of Baptism	Place of Baptism	Presented by	Date of Confirmation *(and place if ministered in another parish)* Officiating Bishop

Confirmations

Entry no.	Date of birth	Christian name(s)	Surname *In block capitals*	Address

Parish of ______________________________

in the Diocese of ______________________________

in the ______________ of ______________________________

Insert appropriate local government area

Date of Baptism	Place of Baptism	Presented by	Date of Confirmation *(and place if ministered in another parish)* Officiating Bishop

Confirmations

Entry no.	Date of birth	Christian name(s)	Surname *In block capitals*	Address

Parish of ____

in the Diocese of ____

in the ____________________ of ____

Insert appropriate local government area

Date of Baptism	Place of Baptism	Presented by	Date of Confirmation *(and place if ministered in another parish)* Officiating Bishop

Confirmations

Entry no.	Date of birth	Christian name(s)	Surname *In block capitals*	Address

Parish of

in the Diocese of

in the   of

Insert appropriate local government area

Date of Baptism	Place of Baptism	Presented by	Date of Confirmation *(and place if ministered in another parish)* Officiating Bishop

Confirmations

Entry no.	Date of birth	Christian name(s)	Surname *In block capitals*	Address

Parish of ____________________

in the Diocese of ____________________

in the ____________________ of ____________________

Insert appropriate local government area

Date of Baptism	Place of Baptism	Presented by	Date of Confirmation *(and place if ministered in another parish)* Officiating Bishop

Confirmations

Entry no.	Date of birth	Christian name(s)	Surname *In block capitals*	Address

Parish of

in the Diocese of

in the   of

Insert appropriate local government area

Date of Baptism	Place of Baptism	Presented by	Date of Confirmation *(and place if ministered in another parish)* Officiating Bishop

Confirmations

Entry no.	Date of birth	Christian name(s)	Surname *In block capitals*	Address

Parish of

in the Diocese of

in the   of

Insert appropriate local government area

Date of Baptism	Place of Baptism	Presented by	Date of Confirmation *(and place if ministered in another parish)* Officiating Bishop

Confirmations

Entry no.	Date of birth	Christian name(s)	Surname *In block capitals*	Address

Parish of

in the Diocese of

in the   of

Insert appropriate local government area

Date of Baptism	Place of Baptism	Presented by	Date of Confirmation *(and place if ministered in another parish)* Officiating Bishop

Confirmations

Entry no.	Date of birth	Christian name(s)	Surname *In block capitals*	Address

Parish of ____________________

in the Diocese of ____________________

in the ____________ of ____________________

Insert appropriate local government area

Date of Baptism	Place of Baptism	Presented by	Date of Confirmation *(and place if ministered in another parish)* Officiating Bishop

Confirmations

Entry no.	Date of birth	Christian name(s)	Surname *In block capitals*	Address

Parish of

in the Diocese of

in the   of

Insert appropriate local government area

Date of Baptism	Place of Baptism	Presented by	Date of Confirmation *(and place if ministered in another parish)* Officiating Bishop

Confirmations

Entry no.	Date of birth	Christian name(s)	Surname *In block capitals*	Address

Parish of

in the Diocese of

in the   of

Insert appropriate local government area

Date of Baptism	Place of Baptism	Presented by	Date of Confirmation *(and place if ministered in another parish)* Officiating Bishop

Confirmations

Entry no.	Date of birth	Christian name(s)	Surname *In block capitals*	Address

Parish of

in the Diocese of

in the   of

Insert appropriate local government area

Date of Baptism	Place of Baptism	Presented by	Date of Confirmation *(and place if ministered in another parish)* Officiating Bishop

Confirmations

Entry no.	Date of birth	Christian name(s)	Surname *In block capitals*	Address

Parish of ____________________

in the Diocese of ____________________

in the ____________________ of ____________________

Insert appropriate local government area

Date of Baptism	Place of Baptism	Presented by	Date of Confirmation *(and place if ministered in another parish)* Officiating Bishop

Confirmations

Entry no.	Date of birth	Christian name(s)	Surname *In block capitals*	Address

Parish of

in the Diocese of

in the   of

Insert appropriate local government area

Date of Baptism	Place of Baptism	Presented by	Date of Confirmation *(and place if ministered in another parish)* Officiating Bishop

Confirmations

Entry no.	Date of birth	Christian name(s)	Surname *In block capitals*	Address

Parish of

in the Diocese of

in the   of

Insert appropriate local government area

Date of Baptism	Place of Baptism	Presented by	Date of Confirmation *(and place if ministered in another parish)* Officiating Bishop

Confirmations

Entry no.	Date of birth	Christian name(s)	Surname *In block capitals*	Address

Parish of

in the Diocese of

in the   of

Insert appropriate local government area

Date of Baptism	Place of Baptism	Presented by	Date of Confirmation *(and place if ministered in another parish)* Officiating Bishop

Confirmations

Entry no.	Date of birth	Christian name(s)	Surname *In block capitals*	Address

Parish of ____________________

in the Diocese of ____________________

in the ____________ of ____________________

Insert appropriate local government area

Date of Baptism	Place of Baptism	Presented by	Date of Confirmation *(and place if ministered in another parish)* Officiating Bishop

Confirmations

Entry no.	Date of birth	Christian name(s)	Surname *In block capitals*	Address

Parish of

in the Diocese of

in the   of

Insert appropriate local government area

Date of Baptism	Place of Baptism	Presented by	Date of Confirmation *(and place if ministered in another parish)* Officiating Bishop

Confirmations

Entry no.	Date of birth	Christian name(s)	Surname *In block capitals*	Address

Parish of

in the Diocese of

in the   of

Insert appropriate local government area

Date of Baptism	Place of Baptism	Presented by	Date of Confirmation *(and place if ministered in another parish)* Officiating Bishop

Confirmations

Entry no.	Date of birth	Christian name(s)	Surname *In block capitals*	Address

Parish of

in the Diocese of

in the   of

Insert appropriate local government area

Date of Baptism	Place of Baptism	Presented by	Date of Confirmation *(and place if ministered in another parish)* Officiating Bishop

Confirmations

Entry no.	Date of birth	Christian name(s)	Surname *In block capitals*	Address

Parish of

in the Diocese of

in the   of

Insert appropriate local government area

Date of Baptism	Place of Baptism	Presented by	Date of Confirmation *(and place if ministered in another parish)* Officiating Bishop

Confirmations

Entry no.	Date of birth	Christian name(s)	Surname *In block capitals*	Address

Parish of

in the Diocese of

in the   of

Insert appropriate local government area

Date of Baptism	Place of Baptism	Presented by	Date of Confirmation *(and place if ministered in another parish)* Officiating Bishop

Confirmations

Entry no.	Date of birth	Christian name(s)	Surname *In block capitals*	Address

Parish of ____

in the Diocese of ____

in the ____________________ of ____

Insert appropriate local government area

Date of Baptism	Place of Baptism	Presented by	Date of Confirmation *(and place if ministered in another parish)* Officiating Bishop

Confirmations

Entry no.	Date of birth	Christian name(s)	Surname *In block capitals*	Address

Parish of

in the Diocese of

in the   of

Insert appropriate local government area

Date of Baptism	Place of Baptism	Presented by	Date of Confirmation *(and place if ministered in another parish)* Officiating Bishop

Confirmations

Entry no.	Date of birth	Christian name(s)	Surname *In block capitals*	Address

Parish of

in the Diocese of

in the   of

Insert appropriate local government area

Date of Baptism	Place of Baptism	Presented by	Date of Confirmation *(and place if ministered in another parish)* Officiating Bishop

Confirmations

Entry no.	Date of birth	Christian name(s)	Surname *In block capitals*	Address

Parish of ______________________________

in the Diocese of ______________________________

in the ______________ of ______________________________

Insert appropriate local government area

Date of Baptism	Place of Baptism	Presented by	Date of Confirmation *(and place if ministered in another parish)* Officiating Bishop

Confirmations

Entry no.	Date of birth	Christian name(s)	Surname *In block capitals*	Address

Parish of

in the Diocese of

in the   of

Insert appropriate local government area

Date of Baptism	Place of Baptism	Presented by	Date of Confirmation *(and place if ministered in another parish)* Officiating Bishop

Confirmations

Entry no.	Date of birth	Christian name(s)	Surname *In block capitals*	Address

Parish of

in the Diocese of

in the   of

Insert appropriate local government area

Date of Baptism	Place of Baptism	Presented by	Date of Confirmation *(and place if ministered in another parish)* Officiating Bishop

Confirmations

Entry no.	Date of birth	Christian name(s)	Surname *In block capitals*	Address

Parish of ______________________________

in the Diocese of ______________________________

in the ______________ of ______________

Insert appropriate local government area

Date of Baptism	Place of Baptism	Presented by	Date of Confirmation *(and place if ministered in another parish)* Officiating Bishop

Confirmations

Entry no.	Date of birth	Christian name(s)	Surname *In block capitals*	Address

Parish of

in the Diocese of

in the   of

Insert appropriate local government area

Date of Baptism	Place of Baptism	Presented by	Date of Confirmation *(and place if ministered in another parish)* Officiating Bishop

Confirmations

Entry no.	Date of birth	Christian name(s)	Surname *In block capitals*	Address

Parish of

in the Diocese of

in the   of

Insert appropriate local government area

Date of Baptism	Place of Baptism	Presented by	Date of Confirmation *(and place if ministered in another parish)* Officiating Bishop